Multicultural Crafts
Kids Can Do!

African-American Crafts Kids Can Do!

Carol Gnojewski

Enslow Elementary

an imprint of

Enslow Publishers, Inc.

40 Industrial Road
Box 398
Berkeley Heights, NJ 07922
USA

http://www.enslow.com

Enslow Elementary, an imprint of Enslow Publishers, Inc.

Enslow Elementary® is a registered trademark of Enslow Publishers, Inc.

Library of Congress Cataloging-in-Publication Data

Gnojewski, Carol.
    African-American crafts kids can do! / Carol Gnojewski.
        p. cm. — (Multicultural crafts kids can do!)
    Includes bibliographical references and index.
    ISBN-10: 0-7660-2457-1
    1. Handicraft—Juvenile literature. 2. African Americans in art—Juvenile literature.
I. Title. II. Series.
    TT160.G58 2006
    745.5089'96073—dc22   2005028668

ISBN-13: 978-0-7660-2457-1

Printed in the United States of America

10 9 8 7 6 5 4 3 2

Illustration Credits: Crafts prepared by June
Ponte; photography by Lindsay Pries. Associated
Press/ Chillicothe Gazette, p. 5; Library of Congress,
pp. 4, 10.

Cover Illustration: Photography by Lindsay Pries.

Contents

Safety Note: Be sure to ask for help from an adult, if needed, to complete these crafts!

Introduction

Throughout the years, African Americans have had to struggle for freedom and equality. Before the Civil War (1861–1865) and during, blacks were slaves on Southern plantations. Though the Civil War fought to end slavery, conditions for blacks did not improve. Leaders began to emerge such as Harriet Tubman. Her courage and bravery led others to freedom through the Underground Railroad.

In the 1920s, an artistic movement came to light, and blacks were slowly gaining acceptance. The Harlem Renaissance gave the world great African-American writers, painters, and musicians. These people told their stories through art.

The 1950s brought the start of the civil rights movement. Women, blacks, and other minorities fought for equal rights. People like Rosa Parks and Martin Luther King, Jr., stood up for what they believed in through peaceful

Harriet Tubman

People today still celebrate the life and work of Martin Luther King, Jr., with a day of remembrance that includes parades.

demonstrations. Their work has helped give many people hope and courage.

History has brought us many great African Americans, some are more famous than others. They each contributed something to the world. Each of these crafts tells a little about a famous or not-so-famous African American that has enriched our lives.

Benjamin's Star Puzzle

Benjamin Banneker (1731–1806) was a colonial farmer who showed his math talents at an early age. Later, he became interested in astronomy and made predictions about the weather by looking at the stars. Banneker also liked to create and solve math puzzles. Make your own Star Puzzle.

What You Will Need:

- yellow and blue craft foam
- pen
- scissors
- glitter (optional)
- star stickers (optional)
- glue
- cardboard
- permanent marker

1. On yellow craft foam, draw a 6-inch five-pointed star. (See page 27 for the pattern.)

2. Cut out the star shape, and trace it onto an 8-1/2 x 11-inch sheet of blue craft foam. Cut the star shape out of the center of the blue foam.

3. Glue the blue craft foam with the star cut out of it onto an 8-1/2 x 11-inch piece of cardboard. If you wish, decorate the blue craft foam with glitter and star stickers.

4. Trace the outline of the star onto the cardboard with a permanent marker. This will form the puzzle board.

5. Use a pen to divide the yellow star into various shapes to form puzzle pieces. Cut out each piece.

6. Trace the pieces onto the cardboard puzzle board. Number the puzzle board and the backs of the puzzle pieces with the permanent marker. This will make it easier for you and others to complete it.

1. Trace a star and cut it out . . .

2. Trace the star shape onto blue foam . . .

3. Glue the foam onto cardboard and decorate . . .

4. Cut the star into puzzle pieces . . .

5. Your puzzle is ready to be put back together!

Latimer Light Bright

Lewis Latimer (1848–1928) was an inventor, draftsman, and engineer. He worked with famous inventors of his time such as Alexander Graham Bell and Thomas A. Edison. He was the only African-American electrician on Edison's research team. In 1881, Latimer patented a process for making carbon filaments in light bulbs. Invent your own Latimer Light Bright design.

What You Will Need:

- black and yellow construction paper
- scissors
- glue
- hole punch
- index card
- white reinforcement circles
- crayons or markers

1. Cut two 4 x 6-inch rectangles out of construction paper. Make one black and the other one yellow.

2. Use the hole punch to evenly punch holes in the black rectangle to make a grid. Make eight holes down and twelve holes across. Space the holes 1/4 inch apart. There should be ninety-six holes in all. You may need to fold the paper slightly to punch the holes in the center.

3. Glue the black grid onto the yellow rectangle.

4. On an index card, make your own design, such as a flower, a boat, or a flag. Decide how many reinforcement circles you will need to make the design.

5. Use crayons or markers to color the reinforcement circles as you wish.

6. Arrange the reinforcement circles on the grid by placing them over the holes. The circles may overlap each other. The yellow paper that shows through from the bottom will make it seem as if your design is glowing.

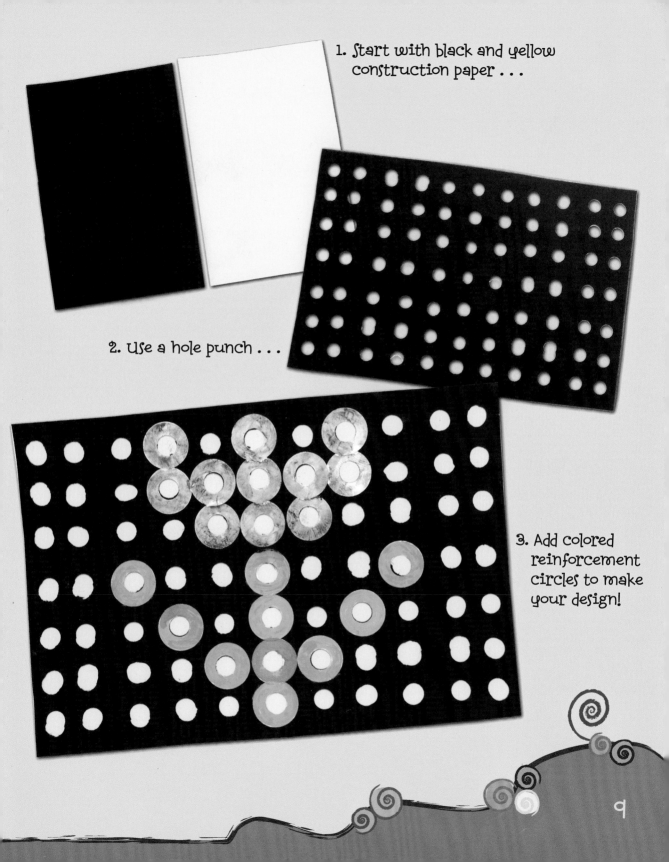

1. Start with black and yellow construction paper . . .

2. Use a hole punch . . .

3. Add colored reinforcement circles to make your design!

Carver Peanut Planters

*George Washington Carver (1864–1943) was an educator and a botanist. He loved plants, and taught farmers in the South how to keep the soil healthy for planting. He experimented with new uses for food crops, such as dyes and adhesives. His research helped to popularize peanut butter. Use peanut shells in a creative way with this planter project. **If you are allergic to peanuts, please do not do this craft.***

What You Will Need:

- whole peanuts in the shell
- poster paint
- paintbrushes
- colored sand
- herb or cactus seeds
- plant mister

1. Carefully split peanut shells in half the long way and remove the peanuts.

2. Use small paintbrushes to paint the insides and outsides of the shells with various colors of poster paint. Let the paint dry.

3. Fill shell halves with colored sand. Add a few herb or cactus seeds to each shell half and cover with more colored sand.

4. Use a plant mister to moisten the sand. Place the planters in a sunny window.

5. When the seeds sprout, put the peanut planters directly into pots filled with soil or into a garden.

George Washington Carver

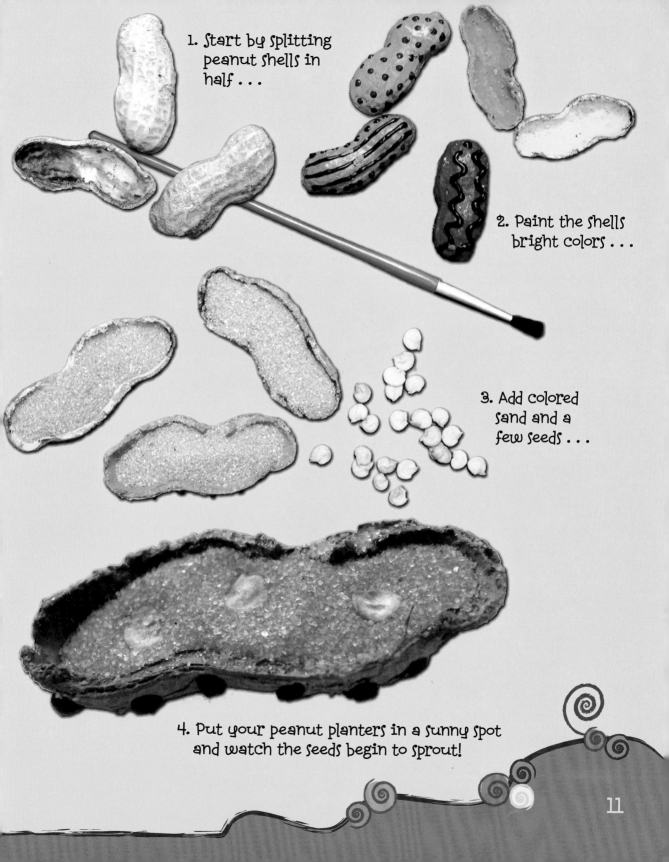

1. Start by splitting peanut shells in half . . .

2. Paint the shells bright colors . . .

3. Add colored sand and a few seeds . . .

4. Put your peanut planters in a sunny spot and watch the seeds begin to sprout!

3-D Globetrotter Stunt Spinner

The Harlem Globetrotters began as a Chicago-area African-American basketball team in 1926. At the time, Harlem, New York, was thought of as the cultural center for African Americans. The reference to Harlem pointed out to basketball fans that the Globetrotters were an all-black team. In 1939, the Globetrotters added comedy and stunts to their playing. Today, the Globetrotters still combine basketball with fun stunts. Create your own off-court magic with a 3-D Stunt Spinner.

What You Will Need:

- white paper
- paper plate
- scissors
- basketball
- orange crayon or colored pencil
- glue
- hole punch
- yarn or string

1. Use a paper plate to trace eight circles onto white paper. Cut out the circles. (See page 26 for the pattern.)

2. Use an orange crayon or colored pencil to make rubbings of the basketball on both sides of each paper circle.

3. Fold circles into quarters and open. Use scissors to cut along one fold to the center of the circle. Fold one cut quarter over the other cut quarter and glue in place. The circle should now have three sides. Do this for the remaining circles.

4. Glue four of these triangular circle pieces together so that they form half of a circle. Glue the other four together to form the other half of the circle.

5. Glue the flat bottom of one half circle to the flat bottom of the other. This will make a complete circle.

6. Use a hole punch to punch a hole at the top of the spinner. Thread yarn or string through the hole and hang.

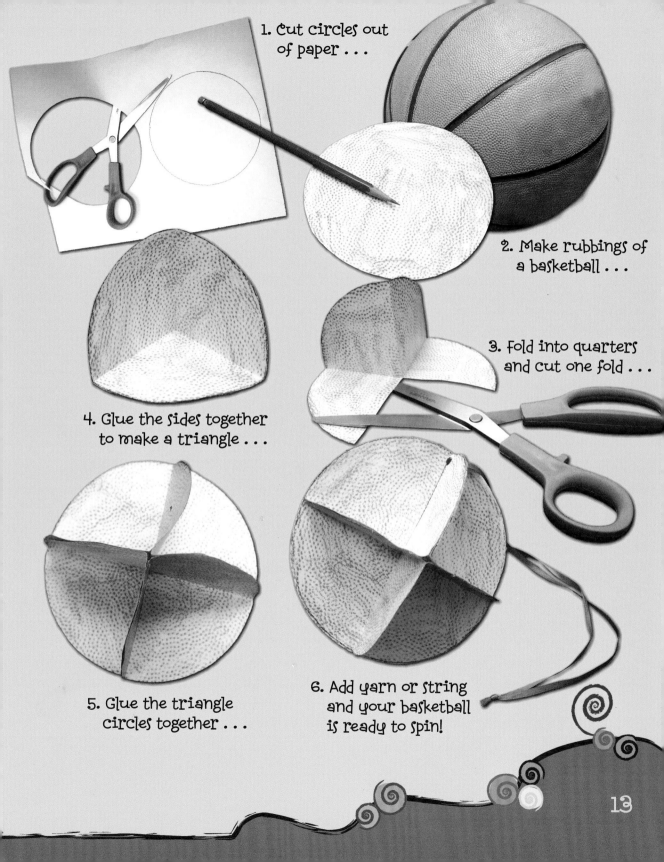

1. Cut circles out of paper . . .

2. Make rubbings of a basketball . . .

3. Fold into quarters and cut one fold . . .

4. Glue the sides together to make a triangle . . .

5. Glue the triangle circles together . . .

6. Add yarn or string and your basketball is ready to spin!

13

Bearden Block Collage

Romare Bearden (1911–1988) was born in the South but moved to Harlem, New York, when he was a child. Bearden became a painter and a songwriter. During the 1960s, he developed a unique collage technique. Bearden took images of African Americans from magazines and newspapers and rearranged them into his own art. He layered the pictures and drew on them. Show your neighborhood by creating your own collage.

What You Will Need:

- magazines (Ask permission first!)
- construction paper
- ruler
- pencil
- scissors
- glue
- crayons or markers

1. Go through magazines and cut out images you like and those that remind you of your neighborhood.

2. On a piece of construction paper, use a ruler to help you draw the outline of your home. Leave room for a sidewalk, yard, or street.

3. Make windows and doors by drawing them, or cutting out and gluing construction paper.

4. Glue images you cut from magazines inside the windows and on the sidewalk, yard, or street. The images do not have to fit in the spaces. For example, a person's head might fill a window. A flower growing in a window box might be bigger than a car on the street. Use crayons and markers to add texture such as brick on buildings, or clouds in the sky.

5. Cut images into the shapes of things you need. For example, a picture of a person could be cut into a drape for a window. A picture of a tomato might be a chimney. There is no one way or wrong way to make a collage!

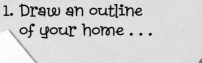

1. Draw an outline of your home . . .

2. Cut out windows and doors . . .

I want to be as big as a tree.

3. Gather up all the images you cut out from magazines . . .

4. Glue the images inside the windows of your house or on the sidewalk, yard, or street!

Ellison's Invisible Postcards

Music and books inspired Ralph Ellison (1914–1994). Through his stories and essays he shared what it was like to be African American. In 1953, Ralph Ellison won the National Book Award for his first novel, Invisible Man. *Make your own symbols to create an invisible message for a friend.*

What You Will Need:

- 5 x 8-inch index cards
- white crayon
- black poster paint
- water
- paintbrush

1. Using white crayon, draw your own symbols, words, or designs onto the blank side of an index card.

2. Turn the card over and write a short note to a friend. If you wish, explain what you have drawn.

3. Ask your friend to thin two parts black tempera paint with one part water. This will make a black wash. Tell your friend to lightly brush the wash over the front of the postcard to reveal the hidden design.

4. Address the note as you would a regular postcard. Add a postcard stamp and drop it in the mail.

Dear Lori,

My message says:

"YOU ARE THE APPLE OF MY EYE!"

From, Lisa.

1. Write your note on one side of the postcard . . .

2. Use a white crayon to write your secret message. Then tell your friend to use paint to reveal the symbols . . .

Dear Lori,

My message says:

TO: Lori Smith
123 Main St.
NEWTON, NJ
00050
USA

"YOU ARE THE APPLE OF MY EYE!"

From: Lisa Jones
345 South St.
Newton, NJ
00050

From, Lisa

3. After the message is exposed, the postcard can be hung up for decoration!

Rita's Murabaraba Word Scramble

Poet Rita Dove (1952–) has received many prizes for her writing. In 1993, at the age of forty-one, she became the youngest poet laureate of the United States. She is the first African American to hold this honor. Shine up your words with this board game activity, based on a South African strategy game called murabaraba.

What You Will Need:

- cardboard
- paintbrush
- markers
- poster paint
- ruler
- scissors

1. Paint a 12 x 12-inch piece of cardboard with light-colored poster paint. Let dry. This will be the game board. Use a marker to draw a large square 1 1/2 inches from the edge of the cardboard.

2. Draw two more squares 1 1/2 inches apart each inside of the largest square. The cardboard will then be divided into a total of four squares. Find the center of the cardboard. Use a ruler to draw a horizontal line and a vertical line through the center. Draw diagonal lines through the middle of the squares so that all corners are connected.

3. With a different color marker, draw small triangles on the corners of the cardboard and at each place where lines intersect.

4. Cut fifty 1-inch squares out of another piece of cardboard. These will be the game pieces. Label the pieces as noted on page 28.

5. Turn to page 29 for rules on how to place the game.

18

1. Paint and draw the game board . . .

2. Carefully cut the game pieces out of cardboard . . .

3. Paint and label the game pieces . . .

4. Get ready for a game of word scramble!

Fab Name Tag

Fab 5 Freddy (whose real name is Fred Brathewaite) helped introduce hip-hop to the world. He hosted the television show Yo! MTV Raps.

Creating a personal identity is a big part of hip-hop and graffiti culture. Graffiti artists in the 1970s made a point of tagging, or signing, their art. Sometimes the tag itself was the art. Tags were a nickname and a number, usually the number of the street that the artist lived on. Take pride in your name and your identity with this Fab Name Tag.

What You Will Need:

- newspaper
- sidewalk chalk
- water
- bowl
- brown paper bag
- scissors
- markers

1. Cover your workspace with newspaper.

2. Place sidewalk chalk in a bowl of water. Let the sidewalk chalk moisten in the water.

3. Cut a brown paper bag down the seams. Place the bag blank side up on your workspace. Think of a "tag" that includes a number that is special to you. Use one color of marker to draw your tag in large, bold, block-print or bubble letters. Make it large enough to fill the paper.

4. Fill in your "tag" with sidewalk chalk. The wet chalk will have a creamy, pastelike texture. Apply it thickly. When it dries, the chalk will have an air-brushed or spray-painted effect. If you wish, use markers to add symbols, words, scribbles, and crossed-out words.

1. Soak sidewalk chalk in a bowl of water . . .

2. Use markers to draw the outline of your "tag" . . .

3. Fill in with the chalk, and your tag is ready for display!

Harriet's Personal Progress Rail

Born into slavery in the South, Harriet Tubman (1820–1913) escaped to the North with the help of abolitionists, people who wanted to end slavery. The route she took was called the Underground Railroad. It was a series of secret hiding places such as houses, tunnels, and roads. Tubman became a leader of the Underground Railroad and returned to the South many times to rescue slaves. Make a railroad track to show the progress you have made in your life.

What You Will Need:

- 2 dowels or sticks
- craft sticks
- glue
- markers
- poster paint (optional)

1. On craft sticks, write the names of people who have helped you in your life. Or write the special events that have happened in your life. You may even want to write some of your goals for the future.

2. Place two dowels vertically so that they are parallel to each other. If you wish, paint them. Let dry.

3. Place the craft sticks in order, starting at the bottom with the events that happened first. Place your goals at the top.

4. Glue the craft sticks onto the dowels like railroad ties on railroad tracks. Let dry.

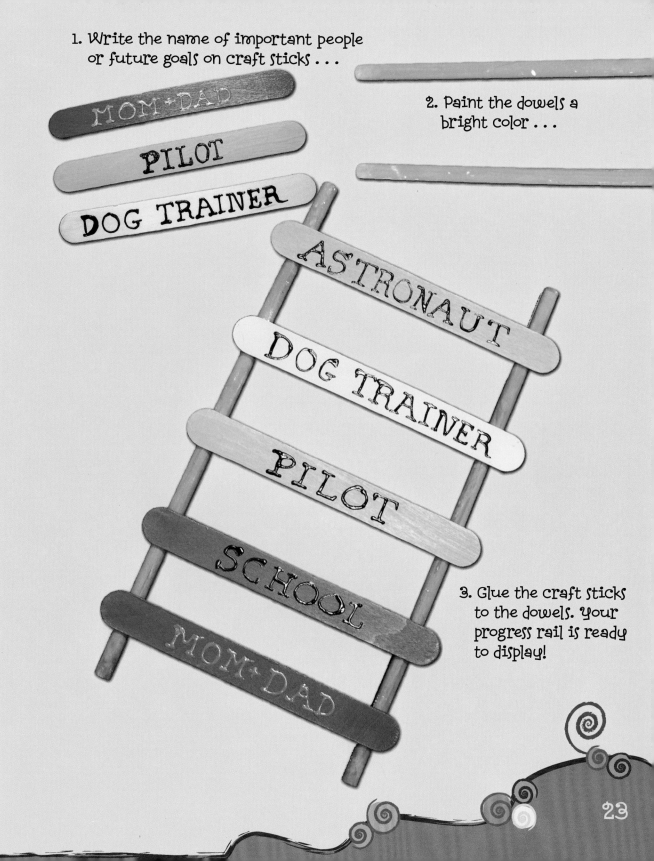

1. Write the name of important people or future goals on craft sticks...

MOM·DAD
PILOT
DOG TRAINER

2. Paint the dowels a bright color...

ASTRONAUT
DOG TRAINER
PILOT
SCHOOL
MOM·DAD

3. Glue the craft sticks to the dowels. Your progress rail is ready to display!

Bob's Commutative Bracelet

Bob Moses (1935–   ) is an educator and an activist who took part in the civil rights movement during the 1960s. Also, a philosopher and a mathematician, Bob Moses later founded the Algebra Project. This education project helps students learn math skills. Use your math skills to make the following bead bracelet.

What You Will Need:

- paper
- pencil
- yarn or ribbon
- scissors
- beads

1. Write the following algebra property on paper: $a + b = b + a$. It is called the additive commutative property.

2. Make a color pattern for your bracelet using this equation. Choose two colors of beads. For example, if "a" stands for yellow, "b" would stand for a different color, such as red (a=yellow; b=red).

3. Decide how many beads of each color you would like the bracelet to have. You might decide to have 6 yellow (a) beads and 5 red (b) beads. Rewrite the equation to match your choices. The equation would read $6a + 5b = 5b + 6a$.

4. Cut a 10-inch length of yarn or ribbon. Find the center of the yarn.

5. Begin adding the beads to one half of the yarn, working from the left side. Using the above pattern, add five red beads first. Then add six yellow beads.

6. Add beads to the right side of the yarn. Using the above pattern, add five red beads first, and then six yellow beads. The pattern of the bracelet should match the equation, with an equal number of beads on both halves.

7. Tie the ends of the bracelet together and wear it.

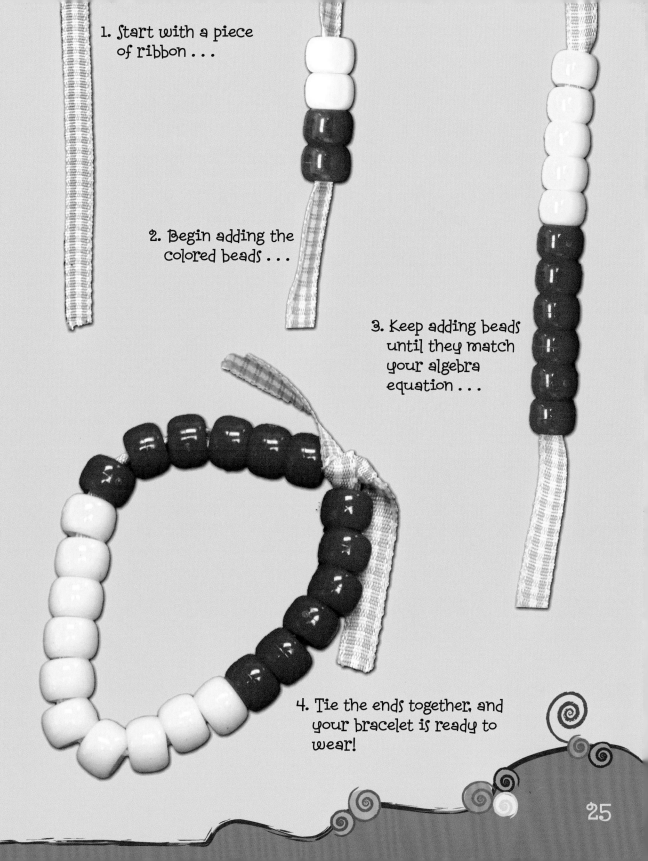

1. Start with a piece of ribbon . . .

2. Begin adding the colored beads . . .

3. Keep adding beads until they match your algebra equation . . .

4. Tie the ends together, and your bracelet is ready to wear!

25

Patterns

Use a copier to enlarge or shrink the design to the size you want.

Use tracing paper to copy the patterns on these pages. Ask an adult to help you cut and trace the shapes onto construction paper.

3-D Globetrotter Stunt Spinner

At 100%

Benjamin's Star Puzzle

Enlarge by 123%

Rita's Murabaraba Word Scramble Game Pieces

For each letter, make the number of game pieces stated. For example, make three games pieces with the letter "e" on each, make two game pieces with the letter "h" on each, and so on.

LETTER	NUMBER OF PIECES	LETTER	NUMBER OF PIECES
e	3	f	2
t	3	p	2
a	3	b	2
i	3	u	1
s	3	g	1
o	3	w	1
n	3	y	1
r	3	v	1
h	2	k	1
d	2	j	1
l	2	q	1
c	2	x	1
m	2	z	1

Game Rules

Rules for playing
Rita's Murabaraba Word Scramble

1. Play with up to four players. Turn over game pieces so that the letters do not show.

2. Each player will select five pieces at a time.

3. Words must be laid down on the triangles and can run forwards, backwards, diagonal, and across.

4. After each play, take more pieces so that you always have five at any given time.

5. Play until the game board is filled or you cannot make any more words.

Reading About

Books

Blue, Rose, and Corinne J. Naden. *Benjamin Banneker: Mathematician and Stargazer*. Brookfield, Conn.: Millbrook Press, 2001.

Greenberg, Jan. *Romare Bearden: Collage of Memories*. New York: Harry N. Abrams, 2003.

McKissack, Patricia, and Fredrick McKissack. *George Washington Carver: The Peanut Scientist*. Berkeley Heights, N.J.: Enslow Publishers, Inc., 2002.

Raatma, Lucia. *The Harlem Renaissance: A Celebration of Creativity*. Chanhassen, Minn.: Child's World, 2003.

Rustad, Martha E. H. *Harriet Tubman*. Mankato: Minn.: Pebble Books, 2002.

Internet Addresses

George Washington Carver: Coloring and Activity Book

<http://www.usda.gov/oo/colorbook.htm>

Learn more and play games at this site from the United States Department of Agriculture.

Harlem Globetrotters: Kids Court

<http://www.harlemglobetrotters.com/kidscourt/>

Learn about the Harlem Globetrotters, play games, and more!

Index